20TH CENTURY SCIENCE AND TECHNOLOGY

1900-20

A SHRINKING WORLD

Please visit our web site at: www.garethstevens.com
For a free color catalog describing Gareth Stevens' list of high-quality books and multimedia programs, call 1-800-542-2595 (USA) or 1-800-461-9120 (Canada). Gareth Stevens Publishing's Fax: (414) 332-3567.

Library of Congress Cataloging-in-Publication Data

Parker, Steve.
1900-20: a shrinking world / by Steve Parker. — North American ed.
p. cm. — (20th century science and technology)
Includes bibliographical references and index.
ISBN 0-8368-2942-5 (lib. bdg.)
1. Science—History—20th century—Juvenile literature. 2. Technology—History—20th century—Juvenile literature. [1. Science—History—20th century. 2. Technology—History—20th century. 3. Technological innovations. 4. Inventions—History—20th century.] I. Title.
Q125.P325 2001
509.041—dc21 2001020782

This North American edition first published in 2001 by
Gareth Stevens Publishing
A World Almanac Education Group Company
330 West Olive Street, Suite 100
Milwaukee, WI 53212 USA

Designers: Jenny Skelly and Aarti Parmar
Editor: James Pickering
Picture Research: Brooks Krikler Research

Gareth Stevens Editor: Dorothy L. Gibbs

Photo Credits:
Abbreviations: (t) top, (m) middle, (b) bottom, (l) left, (r) right

Corbis: pages 5(t), 13(t), 21, 23(t).
Tom Donovan Military Books: pages 4-5(b), 8(b).
Mary Evans Picture Library: cover (br), pages 4-5(t), 7(all), 8(t), 9(both), 10-11, 11, 12, 12-13, 13(b), 20, 22, 24(both), 27(bl, br), 28(t, br).
Hulton Getty Collection: cover (m), pages 5(b), 14(both), 14-15, 15, 16(both), 16-17, 17, 18, 18-19, 20-21, 22-23, 23(br), 24-25, 25(t), 26(t), 27(t), 28(m, bl).
Science & Society: pages 26-27, 29.
Solution Pictures: page 10(b).

Printed in the United States of America

1 2 3 4 5 6 7 8 9 05 04 03 02 01

20TH CENTURY SCIENCE AND TECHNOLOGY

1900-20
A SHRINKING WORLD

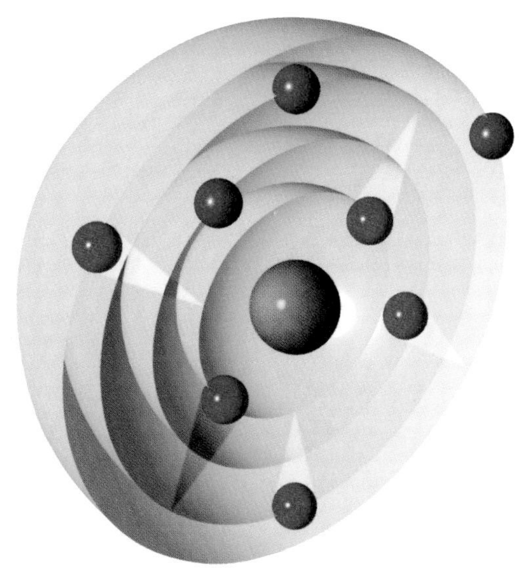

Steve Parker

Gareth Stevens Publishing
A WORLD ALMANAC EDUCATION GROUP COMPANY

CONTENTS

At the dawn of the twentieth century, only balloons and airships traveled the skies. By 1920, John Alcock and Arthur Brown had flown an airplane across the Atlantic Ocean — although they had a rather bumpy landing!

World War I was the first military conflict to use engine power and motorized vehicles instead of just people and horses.

A SCIENTIFIC CENTURY

In our modern world of the Internet, mobile phones, routine satellite launches, and daily heart transplants, imagining a time with no televisions, radios, washing machines, aircraft, or antibiotic drugs is difficult. That time was just one hundred years ago. Back then, only a few rich and important people had electricity in their homes or owned automobiles. The first two decades of the twentieth century saw astonishing changes in daily life. The changes were due mainly to the progress of science and technology. One major invention, the factory, brought huge changes. With assembly lines and mass-production methods, factories churned out millions of new products, and prices dropped. Soon, all kinds of machines and gadgets found their way into everybody's lives. Sadly, from 1914 to 1918, World War I proved true the idea that a military conflict speeds up scientific progress. By 1920, however, a more peaceful scientific era had arrived.

In 1907, the science of electronics leaped ahead with the invention of the triode vacuum radio tube. These tubes were soon being mass-produced.

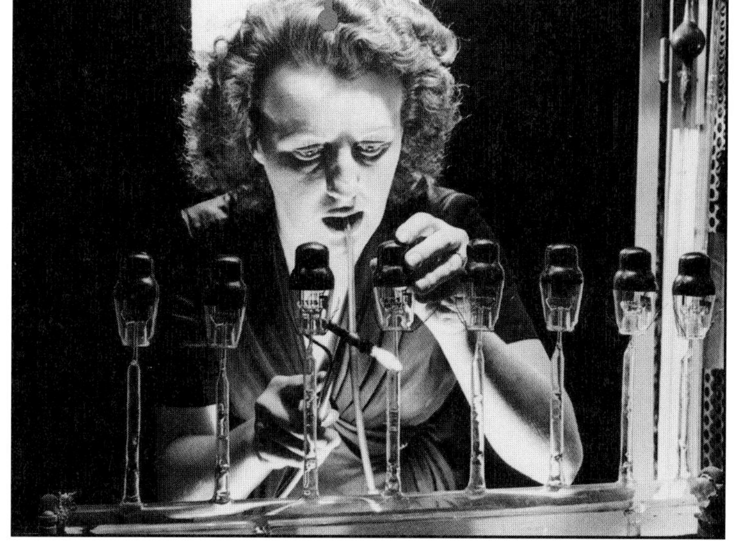

Photography was only for wealthy experts until the Kodak company introduced its easy-to-use "Brownie" snapshot camera in 1900.

BIG IDEAS

Between 1900 and 1920, some of the biggest scientific ideas involved the smallest particles of the Universe — atoms. At least, most scientists of the time thought atoms were the smallest particles. As they experimented, however, using new, high-powered electrical equipment, they discovered that atoms were not the smallest particles.

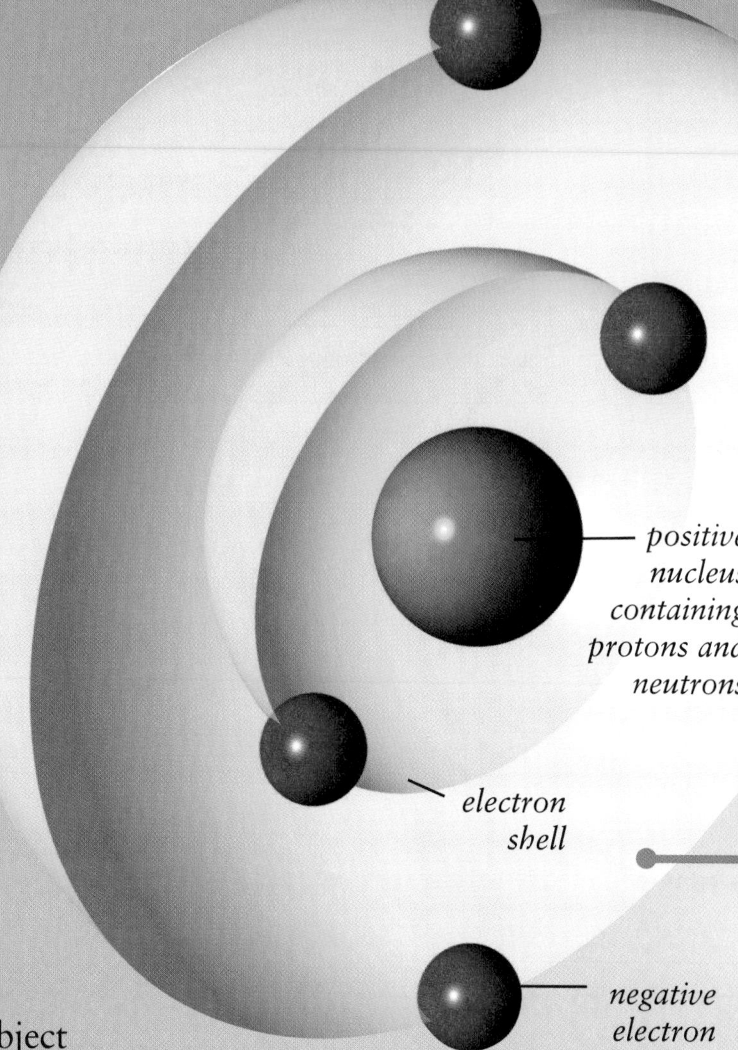

INSIDE THE ATOM

By about 1910, scientists realized that atoms were made of even smaller particles: protons with a positive electrical charge, electrons with a negative charge, and neutrons with no electrical charge. How these particles were arranged in an atom was the subject of many theories and arguments. Ernest Rutherford suggested that protons and neutrons were grouped together in a central area called a nucleus, while electrons whizzed around the nucleus like planets around the Sun. Niels Bohr thought that electrons stayed at certain distances from the nucleus, moving in regions called shells, but sometimes jumping from shell to shell.

THE RAISIN PUDDING THEORY

When British physicist Joseph John Thomson (1856–1940) discovered electrons in 1897, he described an atom as an atmosphere of positive charge with electrons scattered in it like raisins in a pudding. Around 1900, Thomson's theory was one of the main ideas for the structure of atoms.

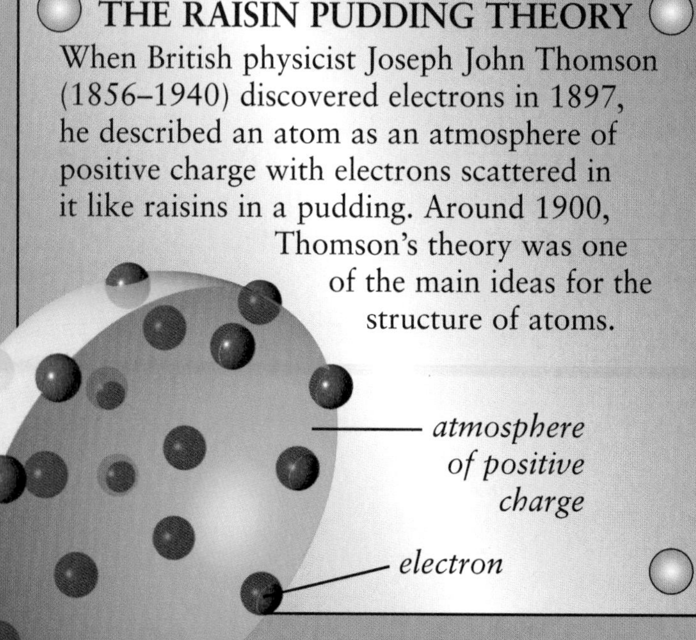

Ernest Rutherford (1871–1937), a British physicist, discovered protons and, in 1911, was the first to suggest that atoms had a dense central area, or nucleus. In 1919, his nuclear research team was the first to split apart an atom.

Danish physicist Niels Bohr (1885–1962) said that electrons did not wander freely in an atom, but stayed at fixed distances from the nucleus. Bohr's idea is the theory of atomic structure used today.

EINSTEIN AND RELATIVITY

From the late 1600s, scientists had used the ideas of Isaac Newton to explain gravity, energy, and how objects, from atoms to planets, move. In 1905, Albert Einstein (1879–1955) wrote an article about "special relativity" that changed the views on these topics forever. In 1915, another article by Einstein on general relativity stated that almost nothing, not even time, is constant. The only constant quantity is the speed of light. Everything else is relative, depending, in particular, on speed. As an object moves faster, time passes slower. Relativity also claims that very strong gravity, such as the gravity near a star, can "bend" space, making straight lines curve.

According to Einstein's theories of relativity, light rays from a distant star bend as they pass close to the Sun.

Star 1 is here.

Star 1 looks as if it is here.

Light from Star 1 is bent by the gravity of Star 2.

Star2

The gravity of Star 2 distorts space and time around it.

WORLD SCIENCE

When World War I began, in 1914, military forces had several new types of machines and technologies that could help them win. In past centuries, wars were fought mainly with people and guns and were a matter of planning and tactics. In the twentieth century, scientific research sped up enormously, with the belief that victory would come to the side that had the most modern and technologically advanced weapons.

The assembly line developed in 1913 for the mass production of cars was also efficient for the mass production of war equipment and munitions.

ON LAND

The tank, a new type of land vehicle, had crawler tracks that were originally invented for farm tractors, to provide better movement on muddy fields. Tanks were powered by diesel engines, developed in the 1890s, and were protected by a new type of very hard steel known as armor plating.

Tanks first saw military action in northern France at the Battle of the Somme in 1916. Their crawler, or caterpillar, tracks could cross mud and trenches.

A British cruiser, the HMS Birmingham, *rams a German U15 submarine (1914). Submarines were effective secret weapons at sea. Early military submarines had diesel engines or electric motors.*

AT SEA

By 1900, ships were powered by steam or diesel engines instead of sails, but the war demanded even faster sea power. The steam turbine offered a new type of propulsion that had been in use since the 1880s to turn generators in electricity power stations. Quickly adapted for ships, the turbine's high-pressure jets of steam blew against the angled blades of a ship's propeller, making the propeller spin with great speed and power. In 1906, the British battleship *Dreadnought* established another new trend in sea power. It had a few large guns that were mounted in swiveling turrets and could be tilted up or down.

IN THE AIR

At the start of World War I, aircraft were used for carrying messages and for reconnaissance, or locating an enemy's position. Only four years later, fighter planes and bombers armed with machine guns and mass explosives were waging aerial warfare on enemy ground troops and on each other. All aircraft at the time were powered by internal combustion gasoline engines, but, because of the war, their speed and power increased tremendously. The first plane-to-plane battle was in October 1914. It involved a Voison LA III with a top speed of 68 miles (110 kilometers) per hour. Three years later, a smaller plane, the SPAD XIII, flew twice as fast. The interrupter was another advancement in aerial warfare. It allowed an aircraft's machine gun to fire directly at an enemy plane without hitting its own propeller. The machine gun was right next to the pilot, so it could be aimed more accurately.

fighter planes in a 1918 dogfight

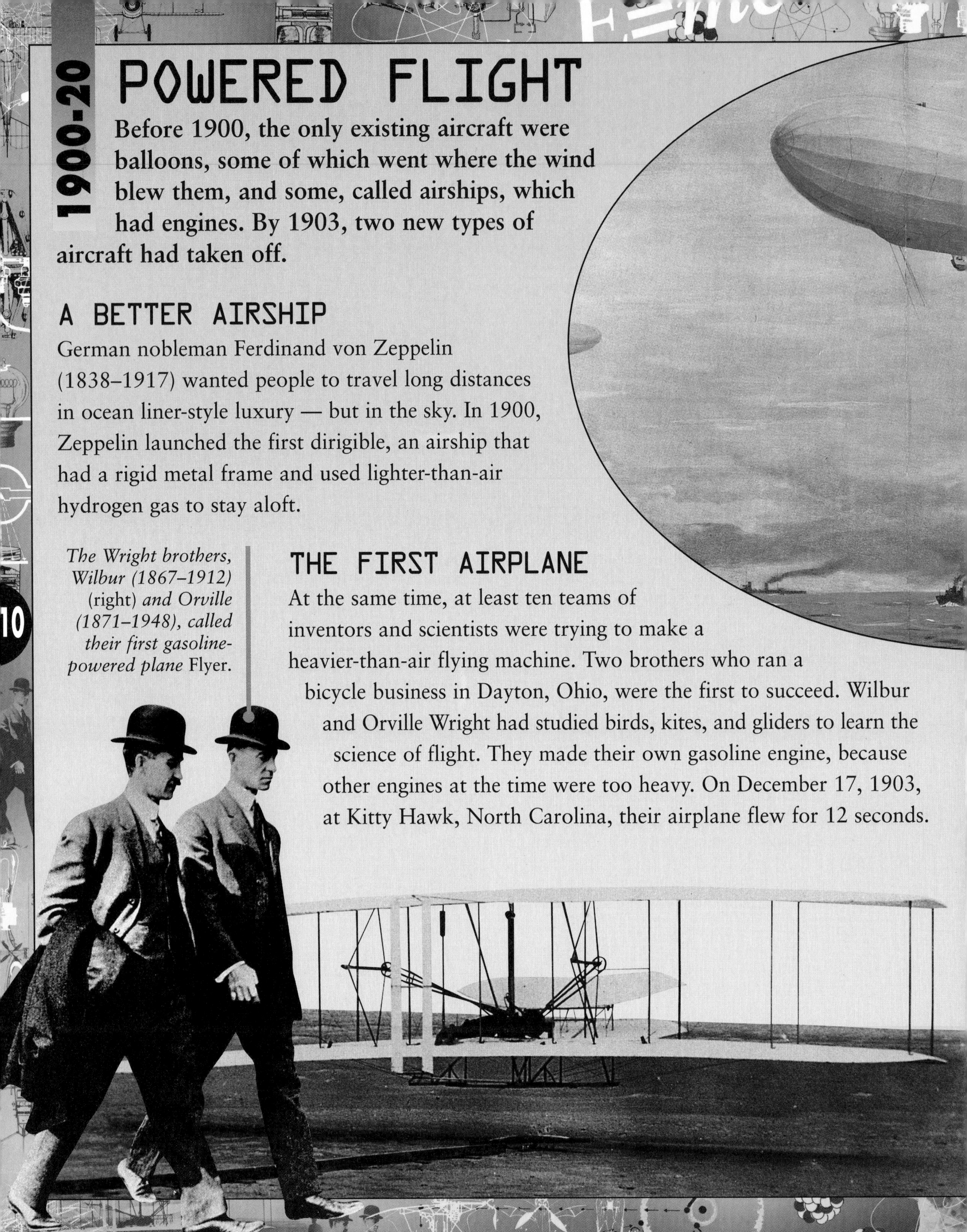

1900-20

POWERED FLIGHT

Before 1900, the only existing aircraft were balloons, some of which went where the wind blew them, and some, called airships, which had engines. By 1903, two new types of aircraft had taken off.

A BETTER AIRSHIP

German nobleman Ferdinand von Zeppelin (1838–1917) wanted people to travel long distances in ocean liner-style luxury — but in the sky. In 1900, Zeppelin launched the first dirigible, an airship that had a rigid metal frame and used lighter-than-air hydrogen gas to stay aloft.

The Wright brothers, Wilbur (1867–1912) (right) *and Orville (1871–1948), called their first gasoline-powered plane* Flyer.

THE FIRST AIRPLANE

At the same time, at least ten teams of inventors and scientists were trying to make a heavier-than-air flying machine. Two brothers who ran a bicycle business in Dayton, Ohio, were the first to succeed. Wilbur and Orville Wright had studied birds, kites, and gliders to learn the science of flight. They made their own gasoline engine, because other engines at the time were too heavy. On December 17, 1903, at Kitty Hawk, North Carolina, their airplane flew for 12 seconds.

Large, rigid airships became known as "zeppelins," after their inventor. Although they were luxurious and faster than land or sea travel, they were easily grounded or damaged by bad weather, and the hydrogen gas inside them easily caught fire.

THE FIRST EPIC FLIGHT

The first powered flight in Europe was not until 1906. In 1909, an air show near Reims, France, featured 38 aircraft. Only 23 of them managed to take off, but the event made aviation a serious science and industry. In July of that year, Louis Blériot flew across the English Channel from Calais, France, to Dover, England, in his *Blériot No. XI* airplane. The flight took 37 minutes to cover 23 miles (37 km). Blériot won a prize of £1,000 from the *London Daily Mail* newspaper and became a world celebrity.

Blériot's aircraft was a monoplane, with two wings instead of a biplane's four.

HOW AIRCRAFT STAY IN THE AIR

The shape of their wings keeps aircraft in the air. Seen from the side, an aircraft's wings are more curved on the upper surface than on the lower, a shape known as an airfoil. As a wing moves forward, air rushes over and under it. The air flowing over the top moves faster than the air flowing underneath the wing. Because faster airflow means lower air pressure, the air pressure below the wing, a force called lift, is higher than the air pressure above the wing. Lift pushes the wing upward and keeps the aircraft in the air.

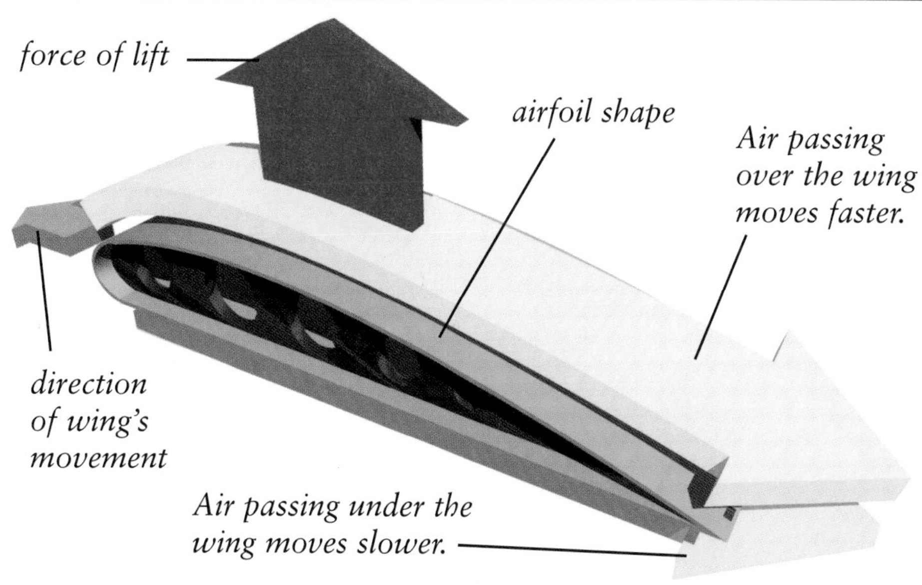

OVER THE WAVES

Many of the technologies we use every day without even thinking about them, especially waves for radio and television, were developed in the early 1900s.

THROUGH THE AIR

The idea of invisible waves passing through air at the speed of light was nonsense to most people in 1900. Italian engineer Guglielmo Marconi sent these so-called "radio waves" over several miles (km), but few people could see how radio might be useful. In 1901, Marconi built a massive radio transmitter in Cornwall, England, and succeeded in sending radio waves nearly 1,900 miles (3,000 km) across the Atlantic Ocean to Newfoundland in North America. The world shrank as long-distance communication became almost instant. By 1915, people could talk long-distance on a telephone.

ACROSS THE WATER

The rise of the airplane had rapid effects on other forms of transportation. In 1907, the first hydrofoil boats sped across water with their hulls lifted clear of the surface on the "water skis" beneath them. The skis had an airfoil shape, like an airplane wing, to produce lift. Hydroplanes were flat-bottomed boats with aircraft-style propellers. They could travel across swamps and reedy waterways where underwater propellers would become tangled.

By about 1920, the propeller-driven hydroplane was a new form of transportation along plant-choked rivers, such as the Amazon River in South America.

MOVING PICTURES

Photography was well established by 1900. Even color photography was available in 1891. All of the pictures, however, were "stills." The first moving pictures were shown in Paris in 1895 by the Lumière brothers, Auguste (1862–1954) and Louis (1864–1948), and became a new form of entertainment — the cinema. In the early 1900s, crowds flocked to watch the magical spectacle of people and events on the big screen. Live shows in local music halls suffered as a result. Technology could bring world-famous film stars, singing, dancing, and newsreels into every neighborhood. Movie cameras and projectors quickly became larger and more powerful.

Before going to England in 1896, Guglielmo Marconi (1874–1937) tested his radio equipment many times in the garden of his family home in Bologna, Italy.

STRANGE PLANES

After the Wright brothers' first flight, other inventors tried to build improved airplanes. One idea was that the more wings an aircraft had, the better it would fly. All kinds of unusual machines were constructed, some with more than fifty small wings, but the Wrights' scientific wind tunnel tests showed that one wing too near another would disrupt the airflow over both wings and reduce lift.

This "multiplane" is being tested in France, c. 1900.

THE PICTURE PROJECTOR

In the 1800s, people paid to watch "lantern slides," transparency images shined onto a large screen by a light projector. With no television and few people who could afford photography, these giant pictures were great entertainment. Movies called for new equipment, such as this Gaumont 1903 dual projector for still and moving images.

film spool, or reel

projection lens

lantern, or lamp

electric motor to wind film spools

electrical connections

ON THE ROAD

Although a small number of automobiles were on the roads in the 1890s, by 1900, cars were being made by the hundreds, each year, in small factories. In 1903, a United States industrialist named Henry Ford (1863–1947) founded an auto company that changed road travel forever.

BASIC BLACK

"Any color as long as it's black," Ford would say. He mass produced cars so ordinary people could afford them. In 1913, Ford set up a moving assembly line so workers could add parts as the cars moved past them. Ford's assembly line cut production time for a Model T by ten hours.

Ford first started to mass-produce Model Ts, or "Tin Lizzies," in 1908. His new production methods were soon used around the world.

GAS, ELECTRIC, OR STEAM?

Not all of the first automobiles were gas-powered. Some had electric batteries; others were steam-driven. In the early 1900s, all three competed for the mass market. The "Stanley Steamer" and several electric cars held the early world speed records, but, in 1913, when a new way to produce gasoline from crude oil was developed, gasoline engines took over.

In 1899, the Jenatzy electric automobile set a land speed record of 65.78 miles (105.84 km) per hour.

THE INTERNAL COMBUSTION ENGINE

A gasoline engine burns fuel inside a chamber called a cylinder, so it is also known as an internal combustion engine. 1. A mixture of fuel and air is sucked into the cylinder (induction). 2. A piston pushes hard against the fuel mixture (compression). 3. A spark plug ignites the fuel mixture (combustion), creating a small explosion that pushes back the piston. 4. Waste gases are forced out of the chamber (exhaust).

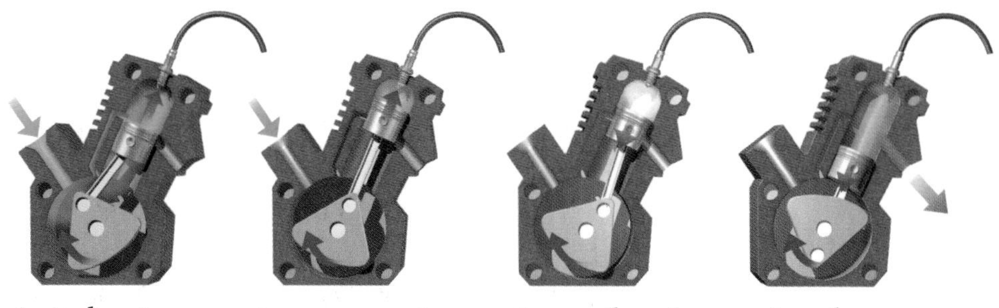

1. induction *2. compression* *3. combustion* *4. exhaust*

PUBLIC TRANSPORTATION

Most people in North America and Europe, even by 1920, still could not afford to buy a car, so public transportation moved from the horse-drawn cart to the engine-driven omnibus — *omni* meaning "all" could travel, although the name was soon shortened to "bus." Streetcars were like one-car trains that ran on rails set into the roadway. By 1914, streets were crowded, and the first traffic lights appeared.

London's first tram, or streetcar, network opened in 1903. Streetcars had electric motors and could switch tracks, like a train, to travel different routes.

In 1919, short trips and outings on motorized coaches, or buses, became a new form of leisure activity. These vehicles had no horses to worry about, and they could easily carry heavy suitcases.

GOING THE DISTANCE

As engines and motors became more powerful and reliable, land vehicles, boats, and aircraft became safer and more comfortable. Long-distance transportation in the United States first took off on New Year's Day, 1914, with regular airline service between Tampa and St. Petersburg in Florida.

The "unsinkable" Titanic *had a double-bottomed hull divided into sixteen watertight compartments that could be sealed off if the ship was damaged. Four of the compartments could flood without putting the ship in peril.*

THE FIRST AIR SERVICE

Airplanes were not the first aircraft to carry passengers on scheduled trips. A German company, DELAG, began international airship passenger flights from Germany to Sweden in 1909. Both airships and the early passenger planes were often grounded by breakdowns and bad weather.

This London-to-Paris mail transport and travel service in 1919 had no cabin heating. Passengers had to bundle up to stay warm in the cold air of high altitudes.

A VERY SHORT SHORTCUT

Ocean travel was slow but more comfortable and reliable than air travel. A coast-to-coast journey in North America, however, meant a very long trip around South America. The Panama Canal, which cut across a narrow stretch of Central America, shortened the journey by almost 7,000 miles (11,300 km). After a false start in the 1880s, construction of the canal began again in 1904 and was completed ten years later.

The Panama Canal is 40 miles (64 km) long and up to 56 miles (90 km) wide. Its six pairs of locks can raise the water level by about 85 feet (26 meters).

SOUNDS IN THE SEA

In 1915, as a result of the *Titanic* tragedy, French scientist Paul Langevin (1872–1946) invented sonar to detect icebergs and other dangers underwater. Sonar sends out "pings" of sound that travel through water at about 5,000 feet (1,500 m) per second. The pings bounce off objects and return as echoes that can be detected by an underwater microphone, or hydrophone. The direction and time delay of the echoes determine an object's position and distance. Sonar stands for SOund NAvigation and Ranging.

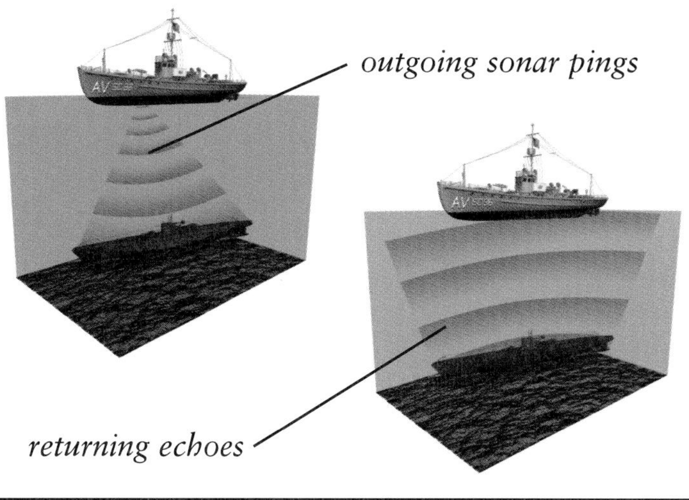

DISASTER AT SEA

The *Titanic* was the largest, most luxurious ocean liner of its time. On its first voyage, in April 1912, the ship hit an iceberg, rupturing five of its watertight compartments, and sank within three hours. Approximately 1,500 people lost their lives.

This farm tractor from about 1905 had a new type of wheel construction called caterpillar, or crawler, tracks. Because driving these heavy tracks required great amounts of fuel, most tractors had ordinary tires with deep treads.

PRODUCT PROGRESS

The electric motors and gas or diesel engines used in vehicles were also installed in factories to power machinery for mass production. Coupled with many kinds of new materials and bigger and better assembly lines, factories were able to produce thousands of products every day, creating a boom in consumer goods.

MATERIALS GALORE

Thanks to product pioneers, such as inventor Thomas Edison (1847–1931) and car-maker Henry Ford, research changed significantly in the early 1900s. Instead of talented but untrained amateurs working on bright ideas alone in their attics, teams of scientists were set up in "inventions factories" to develop new kinds of materials, especially metals for buildings and vehicles.

Assembly lines began with cars, but the idea quickly spread to manufacturing all kinds of products.

The Fuller Building in New York City was nicknamed the "Flatiron Building" because its triangular shape looks like an iron used for pressing clothes. This structure, completed in 1903, stands 21 stories high and is 285 feet (87 m) tall. It was one of the first tall buildings that had a framework made of steel, rather than wrought iron.

NEW ALLOYS

Some of the busiest areas of research involved alloys, which are metals mixed with other substances. One new alloy was stainless steel. Like normal steel, stainless was a combination of iron and carbon, but it also contained the metal chromium, making it very resistant to wear and rusting. British scientist Harold Brearley (1871–1948) first explored the use of stainless steel for gun barrels. Other types of steel were developed for buildings, especially for the metal framework that supports skyscrapers.

First developed as a possible material for rifle barrels, by 1914, stainless steel had become a popular metal for knives, forks, pots, sinks, and other kitchen items.

THE BONES OF A BUILDING

Traditionally, buildings used walls as their main strength. A building's walls supported both its floors and the walls above them. In the 1880s, a new way to support buildings took shape, using metal beams and girders as a framework, or "skeleton," to which floors and walls were attached. In the early 1900s, unusually tall buildings, or skyscrapers, shot up. Between 1914 and 1929, the tallest skyscraper was the 60-story Woolworth Building in New York City, which stands 790 feet (241 m) high.

THE OIL ERA

One of the most important resources in the world today is petroleum, or crude oil. It is used to make gasoline, diesel, and other fuels, as well as lubricants, plastics, paints, dyes, tars, asphalts, preservatives, and hundreds of other products. Since about 1910, the petroleum industry has grown steadily and rapidly, developing new methods to separate, or "crack," crude oil into its component parts, or ingredients.

PYREX

Manufacturing advances around 1900 included a new type of glass called Pyrex. Cookware made of Pyrex could withstand very high oven temperatures.

CHEMICAL FACTORIES

Increasing scientific research created a need for new materials. Some of the most important new materials were chemicals containing nitrogen, such as nitric acid. Nitrogen-rich fertilizers were needed, too, for farming. The Haber-Bosch process made the production of nitrogen-containing chemicals fast and inexpensive.

By about 1913, gasoline was becoming much cheaper to make.

THE HABER-BOSCH PROCESS

German chemist Fritz Haber (1868–1934) was awarded the 1918 Nobel prize in chemistry for his part in developing the Haber–Bosch process, which combined nitrogen (N_2) and hydrogen (H_2) to make ammonia (NH_3). Ammonia is one of the basic substances of the chemical industry. It is used to produce nitric and nitrous acids, as well as a variety of cleansers, disinfectants, synthetic fibers, artificial fertilizers, and refrigeration fluids.

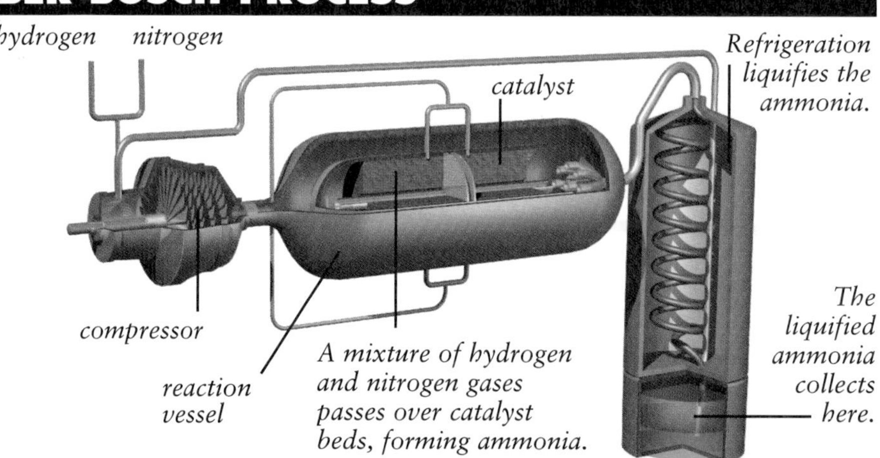

THE HIGH-TECH FARM

For thousands of years, farming depended on animals such as horses and oxen to pull plows and to fertilize the soil with their droppings. Suddenly, engine-powered tractors could work longer hours and without food, care, or stables. Also, one bag of artificial fertilizer had a thousand times more nutrients than animal dung.

"mechanical horse" tractor (1917)

SAFER ELECTRICITY

An increasing use of electrical products created a need for cases, handles, and other parts made from insulators, which are materials that resist the flow of electricity. Most metals, however, are conductors, materials that carry electricity very well. In 1909, Belgian-American chemist Leo Baekeland (1863–1944) invented one of the first synthetic plastics, an insulator called Bakelite.

THICK, DARK, AND WORTH A FORTUNE

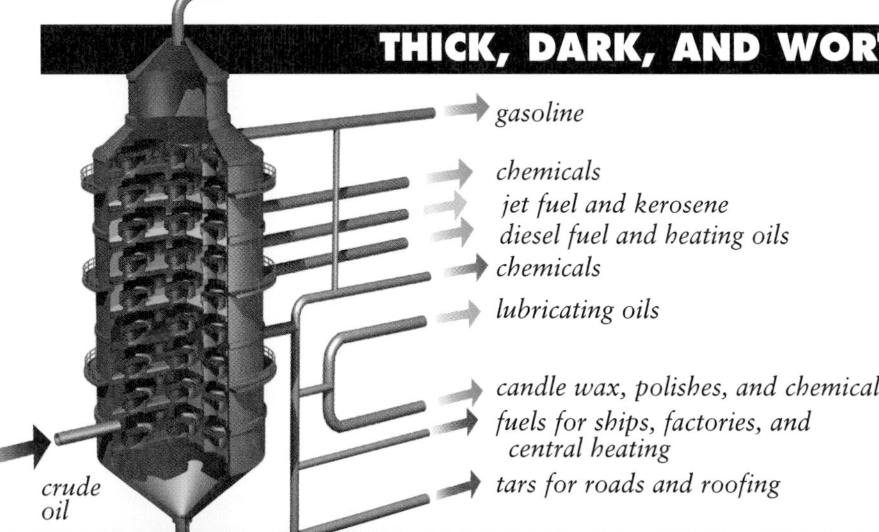

When the first oil wells were drilled in Pennsylvania in 1859, the main substance obtained from the thick, black crude oil was kerosene to burn in lamps. At first, gasoline was a waste product of oil. In the 1900s, however, it was found to be an ideal fuel for engines, and the oil industry boomed. Crude oil was heated to separate it into its many different and useful parts, or ingredients.

By about 1910, the gas street lights in many big cities were being converted to electricity.

ELECTRICAL ENERGY

Electricity is our most useful and widespread form of energy. At the turn of the century, most people, even in big cities, did not have electricity. They used oil or gas lamps and burned coal and wood for heating and cooking. Now, electricity is supplied to almost every home and building in every developed country.

CONSUMER BOOM

From the beginning, electricity was a clean, adaptable, and popular form of power, compared to smelly gas and sooty coal. Along with electricity came a wide range of new consumer goods, such as the electric typewriter (1901), the vacuum cleaner (1901), the washing machine (1908), the toaster (1909), and the refrigerator-freezer (1913). In 1917, Clarence Birdseye (1886–1956) devised a more effective way to preserve food in freezers.

In 1915, using radiotelephony, AT&T succeeded in making the first transatlantic transmission between Virginia in the United States and the Eiffel Tower in Paris, France. Radiotelephony is a way of communicating by radio waves instead of along a wire.

EARLY ELECTRONICS

In 1907, American inventor Lee De Forest (1873–1961) patented a vacuum tube called a triode. The triode worked as an amplifier, using small electrical currents to control much larger ones. It also made electricity oscillate, or reverse direction, very powerfully and quickly, which was ideal for producing radio signals.

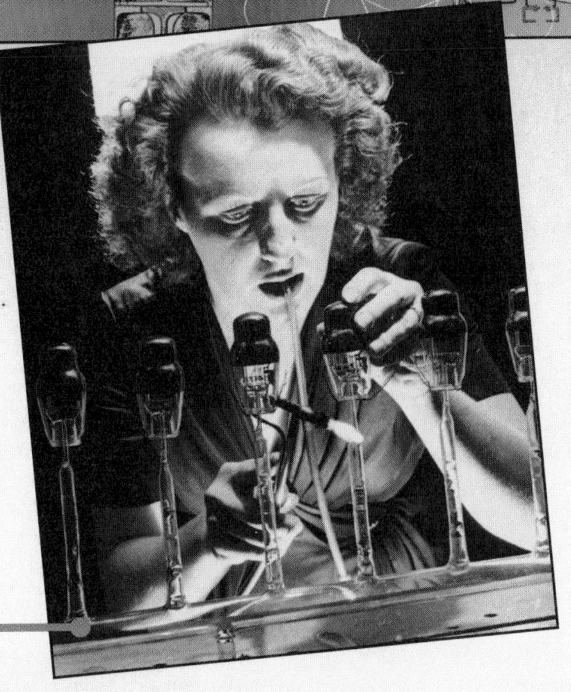

The triode (right) *is one of several types of vacuum tubes. Vacuum tubes were nicknamed "valves" because they control the flow of electricity like a faucet's valve controls the flow of water.*

POWER FOR THE NATION

An electricity power station changes heat energy, such as from burning coal, oil, or gas, into electricity. The heat energy boils water into high-pressure steam that blasts against the fanlike blades of a turbine, making them spin. The turbine shaft is attached to a generator that uses magnets and coils of wire to produce electricity.

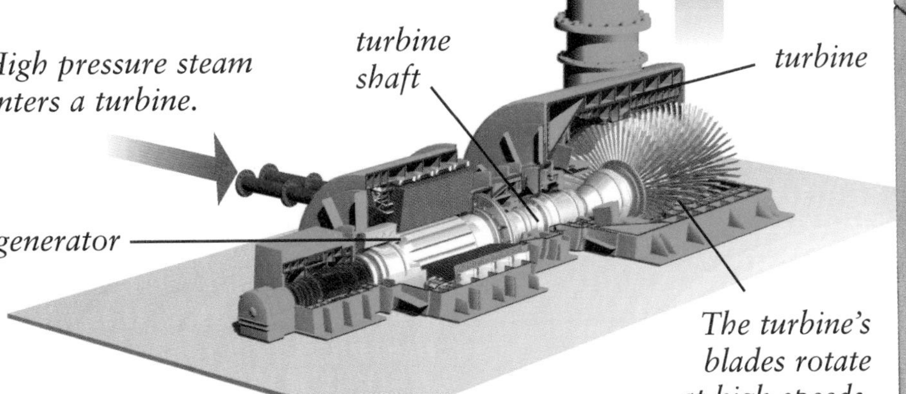

Steam leaves the turbine and goes to condensers for cooling.

High pressure steam enters a turbine.

turbine shaft

turbine

generator

The turbine's blades rotate at high speeds.

The electric range was one of many new household appliances. Models with ovens and heating elements on the cooktop date from about 1919.

MEDICAL MILESTONE

In 1895, a chance discovery in a physics laboratory in Würzburg, Germany, changed medicine forever. Wilhelm Roentgen (1845–1923), a German scientist, discovered some mysterious and powerful invisible rays. He decided to call them X rays until they had a scientific name. We still call them X rays today.

Within weeks after he discovered X rays, Roentgen was working with doctors on possible medical uses.

AN ELECTRIC TUBE

Roentgen was experimenting with a vacuum tube, an electronic device with a glass container from which all air had been removed. Very powerful electricity passed between two contacts, or electrodes, in the tube. This vacuum tube was a simple forerunner of the triode, the cathode ray tube, and, in the 1920s, the television set.

GLOWING CRYSTALS

Roentgen noticed that a piece of paper coated with a certain chemical glowed whenever the vacuum tube was operating. Even if he put a thin sheet of metal between the tube and the piece of paper, the paper still glowed. He guessed that some kind of powerful rays were passing through the metal.

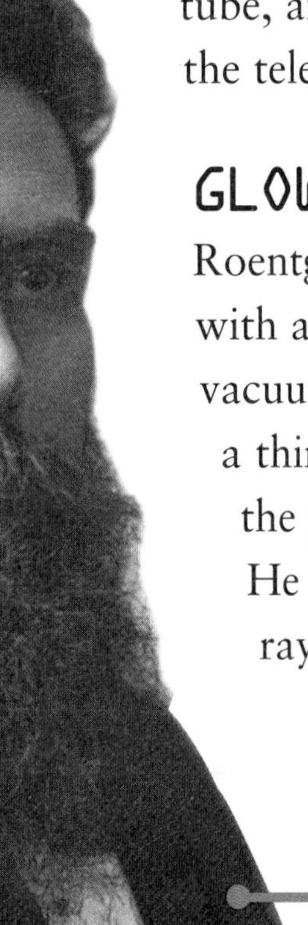

In 1901, Roentgen's discovery of X rays won him the very first Nobel prize for physics.

USEFUL, BUT HARMFUL

Within three months after Roentgen discovered them, X rays were used to look for broken bones, tumors, foreign objects, and other problems inside the body. Before X rays, a body had to be cut open. In 1902, however, X rays aroused suspicion. Some people who had been exposed to them developed health problems, including cancers. Scientific tests in the 1950s proved that large amounts of X rays could be harmful, so they were then used with more caution.

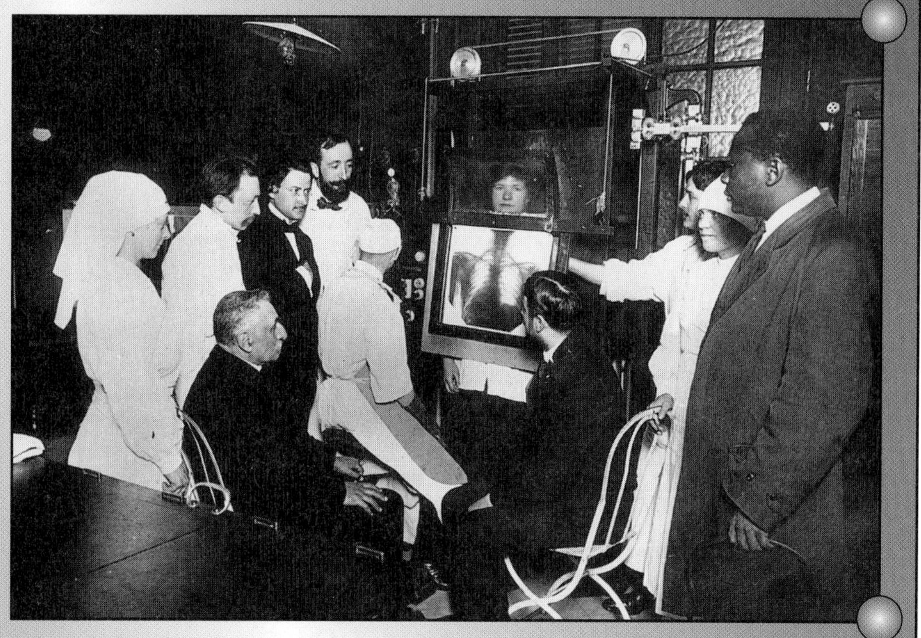

early X ray demonstration

SEEING INTO THE BODY

Roentgen wondered if these rays could pass through a human body. An X-ray photograph of his wife's hand showed that they passed through muscles, blood, and other soft parts, but not through bones. So X rays became a miraculous way to see inside a living person.

Mobile X-ray units carried in vans were used right near the battlefields in World War I to check injuries to troops.

THE X-RAY MACHINE

X rays belong to the electromagnetic spectrum, a range of waves and rays that consists of electrical and magnetic energy. Light rays, radio waves, and microwaves are also part of this spectrum. X rays are made by firing the parts of atoms called electrons at very high speeds against a metal target plate. Lead, a heavy, dense metal, is used as a shield.

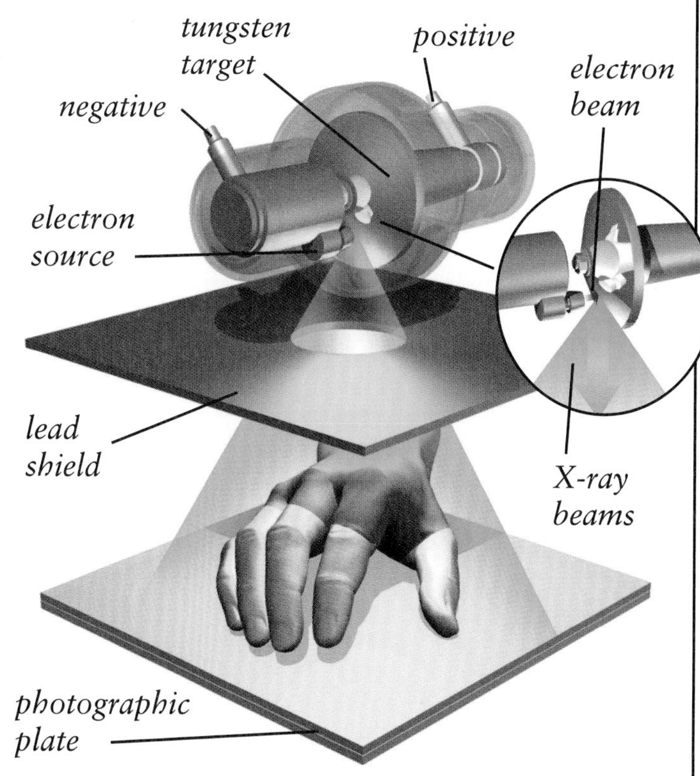

BLOOD TESTS

Blood transfusions are vital in modern medicine. They involve putting the blood, or parts of the blood, of one person into the body of another person. People had attempted transfusions for centuries, even using animal blood, but the patients nearly always died. In 1900, Karl Landsteiner decided to find out why.

MIXING BLOOD

Landsteiner experimented with both his own blood and the blood of five of his colleagues. In some cases, the blood samples he combined in test tubes mixed together smoothly, but in other cases, the mixture formed lumps, or clots. When Landsteiner tested the blood samples for various substances, he discovered four different groups, or types, of blood: A, B, AB, and O. Only certain types could be mixed together safely.

In 1930, Karl Landsteiner (1868–1943), an Austrian physician, was awarded the Nobel Prize in Physiology or Medicine.

THE ABO BLOOD GROUP SYSTEM

The blood types identified by Karl Landsteiner form the ABO blood group system. For blood transfusions, people can safely receive blood of their own type. Type O, called the universal donor, can be given safely to any person. A person with blood type AB, or the universal recipient, can safely receive any other type.

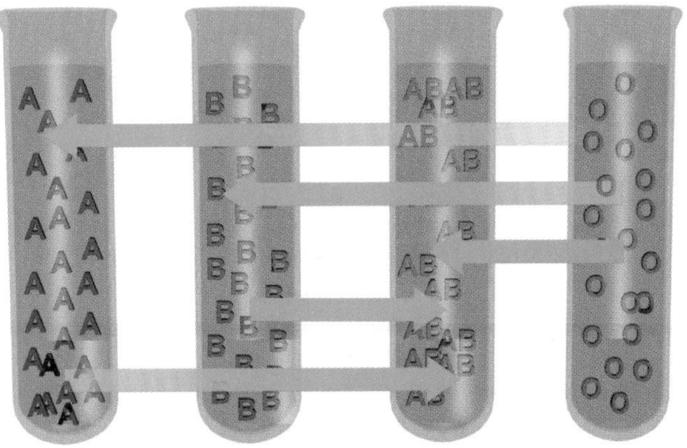

The green arrows show which of the different blood groups can be mixed together safely.

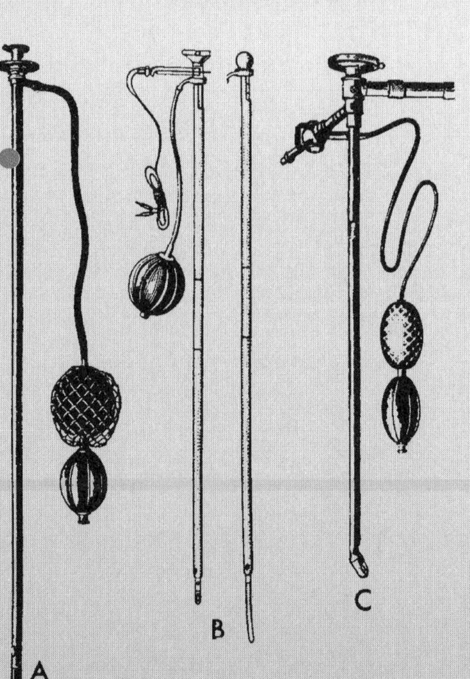

A gastroscope is a device a doctor might put down a person's throat and gullet to see into the stomach. It works much like a telescope. The first gastroscopes were tested in 1911. This collection shows how they changed over the next twenty years.

A DREADED FEVER

Yellow fever is a serious, often deadly, disease found mainly in tropical regions. In 1888, work on the Panama Canal was abandoned because hundreds of laborers died from yellow fever every month. In 1900, a team of U. S. army doctors, led by Walter Reed (1851–1902), began experiments in Cuba. People volunteered to be bitten by mosquitoes, which were the suspected carriers of the disease. The results showed that mosquitoes were indeed the carriers. A great campaign wiped out the insects, and, by 1906, the disease had been conquered.

The mosquito that spreads yellow fever is Aëdes aegypti. *Only female mosquitoes carry the virus because the males do not suck blood. A female bites a yellow fever sufferer, sucks blood containing the virus, then bites someone else and transfers the virus.*

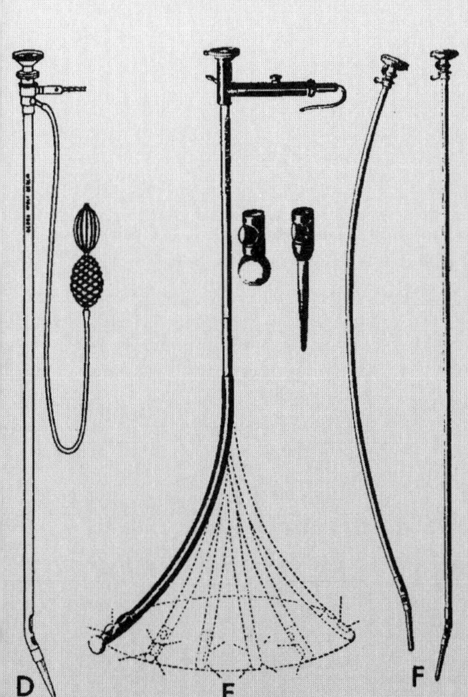

THE RIGHT TO CHOOSE

In the 1900s, women campaigned for equality with men. The campaigns included health and medical issues, as well as the right to vote. In 1914, Margaret Sanger, a New York nurse, invented the term "birth control," saying that women should be able to choose whether or not to get pregnant. In 1920, English scientist Marie Stopes wrote the book *Wise Parenthood* to tell ordinary people the facts about sex and pregnancy.

Marie Stopes (1880–1958)

Margaret Sanger (1883–1966)

GADGETS

With the growth of factories and mass production came hundreds of new machines, devices, and gadgets. Soon, people started buying new products instead of trying to repair old ones. In 1901, disposable razor blades formally introduced a "throwaway society."

SOUND SCIENCE

The phonograph, which played recorded sounds, was invented by Thomas Edison in 1877. In 1888, German-American engineer Emile Berliner (1851–1929) improved its design. Instead of storing sounds as a wiggly groove on a cylinder, Berliner used a flat disk. In 1904, he improved the disk by making it out of a more durable acetate material so it would last longer.

This gramophone phonograph is from about 1891. By 1900, devices like this had electric motors.

Electric food mixers date back to about 1910. They took the hard work out of stirring in the kitchen.

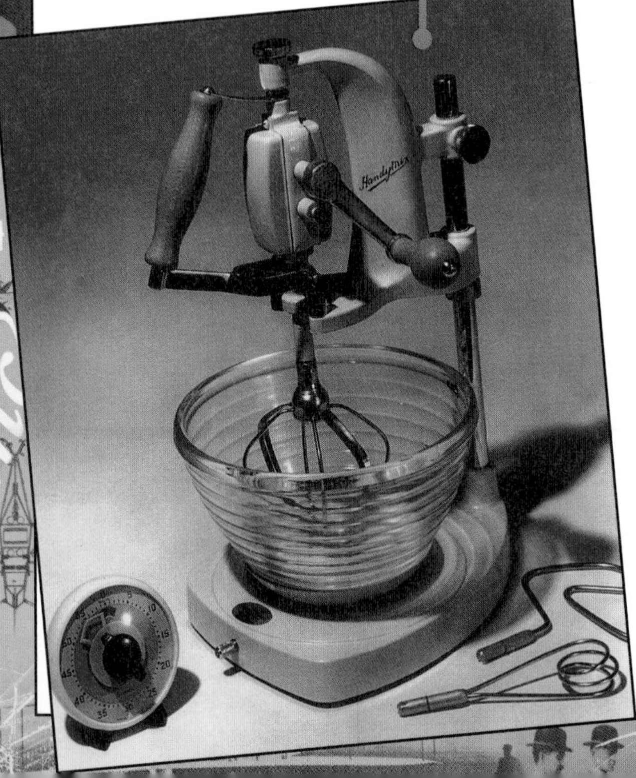

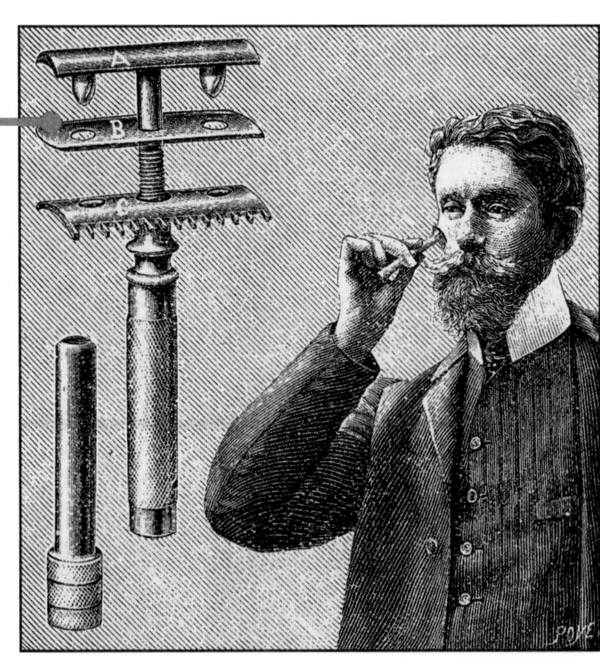

The safety razor, invented by American King Gillette (1855–1932) in 1895, was on sale by 1901. Because the razor's metal blades quickly became blunt, they were the definitive, factory-made "throw-away" items.

A WARM DRINK

The vacuum bottle was invented by Sir James Dewar (1842–1923) of Scotland in 1885. It was used in laboratories to keep liquids hot or cold. In the 1900s, mass-produced versions were used to keep beverages hot or cold.

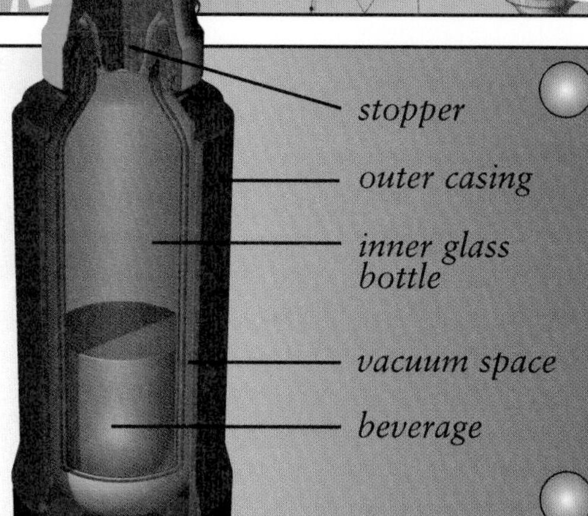

vacuum bottle

COLOR SCIENCE

In 1900, color photography was possible, but it was complicated and expensive until moving picture pioneers, the Lumière brothers, developed the first practical color photography system. They went back to the simple science of how different colors of light can be separated by filters. In 1904, they developed the autochrome process, which gave pictures a bright, "spotty" quality similar to the Pointillist style of painting that was popular in the late nineteenth century.

Old Familiar Flowers, *a 1919 autochrome photo*

THE AUTOCHROME PROCESS

This method of color photography used a flat plate coated with layers of potato starch grains. The grains were dyed orange, green, and violet to act as color filters. The orange grains absorbed all colors of light except orange, and let only orange light through. In the same way, the green and violet grains let only green or violet light through. This layer was coated with a light-sensitive emulsion. Different colors of light hitting the emulsion layer were filtered by the colored grains, tinting different parts of the picture different colors.

1. A glass plate is coated with pitch to make it tacky.

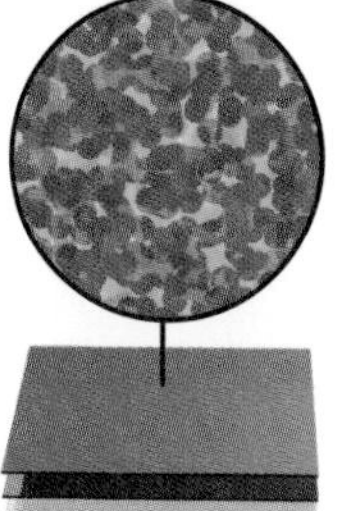

2. Dyed transparent potato starch grains are added to filter colors.

3. Varnish and a light-sensitive emulsion layer cover the grains.

TIME LINE

	WORLD EVENTS	SCIENCE EVENTS	TECHNOLOGY	FAMOUS SCIENTISTS	INVENTIONS
1900	•China: Boxer Rebellion •UK: Labour Party formed	•Hugo de Vries: genetic principles	•Benjamin Holt begins work on "caterpillar" tractor	•Friedrich Dorn discovers radon, a rare gas	•Hubert Booth: first patented vacuum cleaner
1901	•U.S.: President McKinley shot	•First Nobel prizes awarded	•Marconi sends transatlantic Morse code radio signal	•Ferdinand Braun builds a simple crystal-radio set	•Mercury vapor arc lamp •Gillette: safety razor
1902	•South Africa: second Boer War ends	•Neanderthal man reconstructed from fossils	•Robert Bosch puts spark plugs in gasoline engines	•Pavlov: behavioral conditioning with dogs	•Willis Carrier: air conditioner •Lawnmower
1903	•Canada and U.S. settle dispute over Alaska	•Einthoven: medical ECG machine	•Wright brothers complete first powered flight	•Rutherford names gamma rays	•Siemens: electric railway locomotive
1904	•Japan and Russia at war (to 1905)	•Bjerknes: first scientific weather forecasts	•Lumière brothers patent autochrome color system	•George Hale sets up Mt. Wilson Observatory	•Ludwig: photoelectric cell (electricity from light)
1905	•Russia: first revolution	•Einstein: special theory of relativity	•First U-boat submarine launched	•Alfred Binet: IQ intelligence test	•J. Murphy (surgeon): first artificial hip joint
1906	•U.S.: San Francisco earthquake	•Earthquake evidence shows Earth has a core	•Voice and music broadcast by radio	•Marie Curie is Sorbonne's first woman professor	•Light bulbs with tungsten filaments
1907	•New Zealand acquires Dominion status	•Element ytterbium named after a Swedish village	•Paul Cornu: first helicopter flight	•William Thomson (Baron Kelvin) dies	•Hoover: vacuum cleaner •Baekeland: Bakelite plastic
1908	•Austria annexes Bosnia-Herzegovina	•Tyrannosaurus fossils first found in Montana	•Steel-toothed bits used to drill into rock for oil	•Hans Geiger: radiation detector (Geiger counter)	•Model T Ford •Brandenberger: cellophane
1909	•Young Turks overthrow Turkish Sultan	•S. P. L. Sörensen begins using pH scale for acidity	•Louis Blériot flies across the English Channel	•Mohorovicic discovers Earth's "moho" layer	•Enrico Forlanini: first successful hydrofoil
1910	•Union of South Africa created	•Paul Ehrlich describes miracle drug Salvarsan	•Charles Steinmetz warns of power station pollution	•Marie Curie produces a pure form of radium	•First seaplane flight •Wilm: Duralumin
1911	•Chinese revolution; emperor overthrown	•First Solvay Meeting for study of the atom	•Escalators on the London Underground	•Rutherford: "solar system" idea for atomic structure	•First motorized washing machine •Formica
1912	•Balkan Wars (to 1913) •Titanic sinks	•The term "vitamin" is first used	•First tests to prove the existence of cosmic rays	•The Braggs (father and son) measure X-ray wavelength	•Electric blanket
1913	•King George of Greece assassinated	•Bohr: "shell" idea for atomic structure	•Triode vacuum tubes used for long-distance phone calls	•Fabry discovers ozone layer in Earth's atmosphere	•Italy: first geothermal power station opens
1914	•World War I begins •Panama Canal opens	•Rutherford discovers the proton	•UK: first high-tech sewage plant in Manchester, England	•Robert Goddard begins experiments with rockets	•U.S.: first traffic lights installed
1915	•ANZAC troops slaughtered on Gallipoli	•Einstein: general theory of relativity	•First transatlantic telephone call by radio	•Fruehauf: trailers for tractors	•Chemical weapons first used in warfare
1916	•Ireland: Easter Rising in Dublin	•Edward Barnard discovers Barnard's star	•Kotaro Honda: supermagnet alloys	•Ernst Mach dies	•Tanks first used in battle
1917	•Russian Revolution •U.S. enters World War I	•Early predictions of the existence of black holes	•The Gotha: first purpose-designed bomber airplane	•Hale telescope installed on Mt. Wilson	•Clarence Birdseye starts deep-freezing food
1918	•World War I ends •UK: women get vote	•Max Planck: Nobel prize for quantum theory	•First radio link between England and Australia	•Francis Aston builds first mass spectrograph machine	•Alexander Graham Bell improves hydrofoil
1919	•Treaty of Versailles •Nazi Party founded	•Eclipse observations support relativity theory	•Rutherford: "splits" the atom	•Karl von Frisch discovers "waggle dance" of bees	•Daily air flights start between Paris and London

GLOSSARY

ammonia: a colorless, poisonous gas with a sharp, choking odor, which is a chemical compound of the elements nitrogen and hydrogen.

amplifier: an electronic device, especially one that uses vacuum tubes or transistors, that increases the strength of electrical currents.

assembly line: a continuous series, or direct line, of machines, materials, and workers through which a manufactured product passes until it has been completely assembled.

crude oil: the flammable liquid hydrocarbon mixture in Earth's upper layer as it exists in its raw or natural state, before being processed or refined into gasoline, fuel oils, and other petrochemicals.

internal combustion engine: a machine that runs on heat energy created by burning, or combustion, inside the machine, instead of in a separate furnace.

oscillator: an electronic device that periodically reverses, or alternates, the amount or direction of electrical current.

relativity: a set of fundamental scientific ideas that establishes the speed of light as the only constant quantity of the Universe and describes all other natural happenings, including time, space, mass, motion, and gravity, as being variable and relative, especially to speed.

sonar: a method or device that uses sound to detect and locate objects underwater.

triode vacuum tube: a bulb-shaped glass container from which most of the air has been removed, creating a vacuum, and inside of which small metal plates called electrodes control electronic signals.

X ray: electromagnetic radiation with a very short wavelength that can penetrate solid masses.

MORE BOOKS TO READ

Albert Einstein: Physicist and Genius. Great Minds of Science (series). Joyce Goldenstern (Enslow)

The Camera. Turning Point Inventions (series). Joseph Wallace (Atheneum)

The Ever-Changing Atom. Roy A. Gallant (Benchmark Books)

Eyewitness: Electronics. Roger Bridgman (DK Publishing)

Great Discoveries & Inventions (series). Antonio Casanellas (Gareth Stevens)

Machines: Engines, Elevators, and X Rays. Science@Work (series). Janice Parker (Raintree/Steck-Vaughn)

Medical Advances. 20th Century Inventions (series). Steve Parker (Raintree/Steck-Vaughn)

Titanic. Frank Sloan (Raintree/Steck-Vaughn)

Visual Wonders: Ships, Trains, and Planes. Richard Humble et al. (Graphic Arts Center)

The Wright Brothers: How They Invented the Airplane. Russell Freedman (Holiday House)

WEB SITES

Atom Builder: You Try It.
www.pbs.org/wgbh/aso/tryit/atom/

The Model T Ford Club: Kid's Page.
www.modelt.org/kid1.html

The New Light: Discovery and Introduction.
www.xray.hmc.psu.edu/rci/contents_1.html

Take Off! A History of Aviation. *familyeducation.com/topic/front/0%2C1156%2C4-6367%2C00.html*

Due to the dynamic nature of the Internet, some web sites stay current longer than others. To find additional web sites, use a reliable search engine with one or more of the following keywords: *aircraft, atoms, automobile, Einstein, electronics, engines, Henry Ford, Marconi, radio, Roentgen, Titanic, Wright brothers,* and *X ray.*

INDEX